Endangered PENGUINS

EARTH'S ENDANGERED ANIMALS

Bobbie Kalman & Robin Johnson

Crabtree Publishing Company

www.crabtreebooks.com

Earth's Endangered Animals Series

A Bobbie Kalman Book

Dedicated by Robin Johnson
For Melissa, Cindy, Jennifer, and Jeanine, the coolest chicks I know

Editor-in-Chief
Bobbie Kalman

Writing team
Bobbie Kalman
Robin Johnson

Substantive editor
Kathryn Smithyman

Project editor
Kelley MacAulay

Editors
Molly Aloian
Rebecca Sjonger
Michael Hodge

Photo research
Crystal Foxton

Design
Katherine Kantor

Production coordinator
Heather Fitzpatrick

Consultant
Patricia Loesche, Ph.D., Animal Behavior Program,
Department of Psychology, University of Washington

Illustrations
Barbara Bedell: page 18
Vanessa Parson-Robbs: back cover (bottom), pages 10 (left penguin beak), 14
Margaret Amy Salter: back cover (top), page 10 (except left penguin beak)

Photographs
Animals Animals - Earth Scenes: © Mark Chappell: page 28; © Phyllis Greenberg: page 17;
   © Gerard Lacz: pages 18-19
Associated Press: page 30
© Eric Gevaert. Image from BigStockPhoto.com: page 16
Dreamstime.com: © Nicola Gavin: page 11 (bottom); © Eric Gevaert: page 13 (left)
Fotolia.com: James Steidl: pages 20-21 (top)
iStockphoto.com: Andrew Howe: page 23 (top); Stepan JeZek: page 25 (top);
   Nancy Nehring: page 25 (bottom); Patrick Roherty: page 27; Lynn Seeden: page 31
SeaPics.com: © Bryan & Cherry Alexander: page 29; © Marc Chamberlain: front cover, page 22
© ShutterStock.com/Pascaline Daniel: page 9
Other images by Corel, Digital Stock, and Digital Vision

Library and Archives Canada Cataloguing in Publication

Kalman, Bobbie, 1947-
    Endangered penguins / Bobbie Kalman & Robin Johnson.

(Earth's endangered animals)
Includes index.
ISBN 978-0-7787-1863-5 (bound)
ISBN 978-0-7787-1909-0 (pbk.)

    1. Penguins--Juvenile literature. 2. Endangered species--Juvenile
literature. I. Johnson, Robin (Robin R.) II. Title. III. Series.

QL696.S473K337 2007   j598.47   C2007-900529-2

Library of Congress Cataloging-in-Publication Data

Kalman, Bobbie.
   Endangered Penguins / Bobbie Kalman & Robin Johnson.
      p. cm. -- (Earth's endangered animals)
   Includes index.
   ISBN-13: 978-0-7787-1863-5 (rlb)
   ISBN-10: 0-7787-1863-8 (rlb)
   ISBN-13: 978-0-7787-1909-0 (pb.)
   ISBN-10: 0-7787-1909-X (pb.)
   1. Penguins--Juvenile literature. 2. Endangered species--Juvenile
literature. I. Johnson, Robin (Robin R.) II. Title. III. Series.
   QL696.S473K35 2007
   598.47--dc22

                                                                    2007002691

Crabtree Publishing Company

www.crabtreebooks.com   1-800-387-7650

Published in Canada
Crabtree Publishing
616 Welland Ave.
St. Catharines, ON
L2M 5V6

Published in the United States
Crabtree Publishing
PMB16A
350 Fifth Ave., Suite 3308
New York, NY 10118

Published in the United Kingdom
Crabtree Publishing
White Cross Mills
High Town, Lancaster
LA1 4XS

Published in Australia
Crabtree Publishing
386 Mt. Alexander Rd.
Ascot Vale (Melbourne)
VIC 3032

Contents

Penguins at risk

There are seventeen **species**, or types, of penguins. Some scientists believe that three penguin species are **endangered**. Endangered animals are at risk of disappearing from Earth forever. Scientists also believe that another seven penguin species are **vulnerable**.

Penguins need help!

People must protect endangered penguins and other endangered animals. Without help, many of these species will become **extinct**. When you learn more about penguins, you will want to help them survive.

Words to know

Scientists use certain words to describe animals in danger. Some of these words are listed below.

vulnerable Describes animals that may soon become endangered

endangered Describes animals that are in danger of dying out in the **wild**

critically endangered Describes animals that are at high risk of dying out in the wild

extinct Describes animals that are no longer known to live anywhere on Earth

What are penguins?

Penguins are **birds**. Birds are animals that have feathers covering their bodies. They are **warm-blooded** animals. The bodies of warm-blooded animals stay about the same temperatures no matter how warm or cold their surroundings are.

Wings for swimming

Birds have wings. Most birds use their wings to fly, but penguins do not fly. Penguins live mainly in oceans. Their wings help them swim quickly through water.

Up for air

Like all birds, penguins breathe air using **lungs**. Lungs take in air and let out air. Penguins cannot breathe under water. To breathe air, they swim up to the surface of the water.

Most penguins swim about five miles (8 km) per hour. Some penguins, however, can swim up to fifteen miles (24 km) per hour. This gentoo penguin is a fast swimmer.

Penguin habitats

All seventeen species of penguins live in the **Southern Hemisphere**. Most species live in the oceans around South America, Australia, and Africa. These areas are near the **equator**, where it is hot year round. Galapagos penguins, African penguins, and Humboldt penguins live in warm ocean waters around the equator.

Always cold

Some penguin species live in the freezing Southern Ocean around Antarctica. The **South Pole** is in Antarctica. It is cold year round near the South Pole. Emperor penguins, king penguins, and Adélie penguins live in the Southern Ocean.

These African penguins live in the southern part of Africa. African penguins are vulnerable.

8

Penguins on land

The natural place where an animal lives is called its **habitat**. Oceans are just one penguin habitat. Once a year, penguins leave their ocean habitat to lay eggs and raise **chicks**, or baby penguins. Penguins that live near South America, Australia, and Africa raise their chicks on land. Different penguin species raise chicks in different land habitats. These habitats include rocky areas, sandy beaches, and forests. The areas where penguins lay eggs and raise chicks are called **breeding grounds**.

Cold spots

Some penguins that live near Antarctica lay eggs and raise chicks on land. The land in Antarctica is usually covered with ice and snow. Other penguins that live near Antarctica lay eggs and raise their chicks on **pack ice**. Pack ice is made up of huge sheets of ice that float in cold oceans.

These chinstrap penguins raise their chicks on land.

Penguin bodies

Penguins have layers of fat called **blubber** under their skin. Blubber helps keep them warm. Penguins also have two layers of feathers. Next to their skin, they have warm, fluffy feathers called **down**. The feathers on top of the down are stiff. These stiff feathers are **waterproof**. They keep water out.

*Penguins use their powerful **beaks** to catch **prey**. Penguins have sharp, backward-pointing spikes in their mouths and on their tongues. The spikes help penguins hold slippery food.*

Penguins have feathers covering their ears. They still have good hearing, however.

*Penguins have **webbed feet**. Webbed feet have thin skin between the toes. Penguins use their webbed feet to steer and stop in water.*

beak

Keeping cool
Penguins that live in warm ocean waters have thinner blubber than do penguins that live in cold waters. They also have thinner layers of feathers. Having thin blubber and feathers helps these penguins stay cool.

10

Molting feathers

Each year, penguins **molt**, or shed their worn-out feathers and grow new feathers. It takes several weeks for penguins to molt. Penguins must molt on land or on pack ice. They **fast**, or go without eating, while they molt. Molting is important for penguins. By molting, penguins always have strong, waterproof feathers. They need waterproof feathers to survive in oceans.

This penguin has molted a large patch of feathers on its belly.

Penguins preen

Penguins care for their feathers by **preening**, or using their beaks to comb and put oil on their feathers. First, the penguins nudge their feathers into place. They then take oil from body parts called **preen glands**, which are located near their tails. They rub the oil into their feathers. The oil makes the feathers shiny, smooth, and waterproof.

11

Living in colonies

Most penguin species live in groups called **colonies**. Some penguin colonies are small, and others are large. Many penguin **pairs** live in a colony. A pair is a male and a female penguin that are raising chicks. Most pairs have **territories** within the breeding ground. A pair's territory is a small area around the place where the female lays her eggs.

These Adélie penguins are caring for their eggs in their territories.

Nests

Most penguin species make nests for their eggs. The eggs are warm and safe in the nests. Penguins use different materials to make their nests. Some penguins use plant materials. Others make nests out of **guano**, or dry bird droppings.

This penguin has gathered grasses for its nest.

No nest for you

Penguins that live around Antarctica do not build nests. In Antarctica, nests do not keep eggs warm enough. Instead of making nests, Antarctic penguins use their bodies to keep their eggs safe and warm. King penguins and emperor penguins have **brood pouches** on their bellies. A brood pouch is a thick flap of skin. The penguins balance the eggs on their feet and tuck them into their brood pouches. The pouches keep the eggs warm.

The life cycle of a penguin

Every animal goes through a set of changes as it grows. The changes are called the animal's **life cycle**. A chick hatches from an egg. It is covered with down. The chick grows and changes until it **fledges**, or grows a layer of stiff, waterproof feathers over its down. It is now a **juvenile**. The juvenile continues to grow and change until it is **mature**, or an adult. An adult penguin can **mate**, or join together with another penguin to make babies.

The life cycle of an erect-crested penguin

An erect-crested penguin chick grows inside an egg for about 35 days.

*The chick's mother and father take turns feeding it, keeping it warm, and protecting it from **predators**.*

The penguin is mature when it is between two and six years old.

*Soon after fledging, the juvenile penguin enters the ocean. It knows by **instinct** how to hunt for food and swim. Instinct is knowing something without being taught.*

14

Chick care

The adults of some penguin species feed and protect their chicks from the time they hatch to the time they fledge. The adults of a few species care for their chicks for several weeks or months. The parents then leave the chicks before the chicks fledge. They leave the chicks huddled together in groups called **crèches**. A chick in a crèche is safer from predators than a chick that is alone.

*The parents feed their chicks by **regurgitating**, or bringing up, food from their stomachs.*

Food for some

Adults of some species continue to feed their chicks in the crèches. Other species of adults do not feed their chicks. These chicks fast for several months until they fledge. After fledging, the chicks find their own food.

In cold habitats, chicks huddle together in crèches to keep warm.

Penguin behavior

Penguins **communicate**, or send messages, to other penguins. One way penguins communicate is by making sounds. Penguins that live in large colonies make loud **contact calls** to find their partners or chicks. They can find them among the millions of other penguins in the colonies. Penguin contact calls sound like loud trumpets.

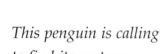

This penguin is calling to find its partner.

Look at me!

Another way penguins communicate is by behaving in different ways. The penguins of some species greet one another by bowing, flapping their wings, or waving their beaks in the air. Chicks touch their parents' beaks with their own beaks to communicate that they are hungry. Not all penguin communication is friendly, however. One penguin may threaten another penguin by opening its beak and pointing it at the other penguin.

These macaroni penguins are threatening each other.

Life in water

All penguins hunt for food in oceans, but different penguins catch different prey. Penguins are **carnivores**. Carnivores are animals that eat other animals. Most penguins eat fish and tiny animals called **krill**. Many penguins also eat squid.

krill

Up for air

Penguins swim quickly when they are chasing prey. They often **porpoise** while they swim. To porpoise is to leap from the water, breathe in air, and dive back into the water. Porpoising allows penguins to get the air they need while they are swimming.

A Humboldt penguin has caught a fish to eat. Another penguin is trying to steal the fish!

Dangers in oceans

Penguins face many dangers in their ocean habitats. One threat is **pollution**. People pollute oceans with oil, chemicals, and garbage. Many penguins die when their wings or feet get caught in floating garbage.

Oil spills

Oil tankers are boats that move oil from place to place on oceans. Oil often spills out of oil tankers into oceans. The thick black oil sticks to the bodies of penguins. The oil ruins the waterproof coating on their feathers. Without the waterproof coating, penguins may freeze to death. When penguins preen their oil-covered feathers, they swallow some of the oil. The oil poisons the birds. Most poisoned penguins die.

Dumping oil

After a load of oil is pumped out of an oil tanker, the ship is filled with ocean water because a tanker without a full tank may roll over in the ocean. The ship then travels to pick up more oil. The water in the tanker is removed before the new oil is added. To protect oceans, people are supposed to pump the oily water into holding tanks, which are on shore. Rather than waiting for the oily water to be pumped into the holding tanks, however, many tankers dump the oily water into the oceans. This water harms penguins and other ocean animals.

Chemicals from factories and farms often wash into river waters that end up in oceans. Over time, these chemicals build up in the bodies of ocean animals, including little blue penguins. These chemicals kill many of the animals.

Dangers on land

One of the greatest threats to penguins is **habitat loss**. Habitat loss is the destruction of the natural areas in which animals live, find food, and have babies. Around the world, people **clear** land to make room for roads, houses, and farms. Logging companies clear huge areas of land and sell the trees to make wood and paper products. Some penguin species lose their breeding grounds when their land habitat is cleared.

Yellow-eyed penguins are endangered because of habitat loss. These penguins lay eggs and have babies in the forests of New Zealand. Large areas of the forests have been cleared, however.

Introduced species

When people move to an area, they often bring animals with them that have never lived in that area. The new animals are called **introduced species**. Animals that have been introduced to penguin land habitats include dogs, cats, rats, pigs, and ferrets. Many of the introduced animals are penguin predators. Penguin **populations** decline when the number of predators in their habitats increases.

Introduced predators such as rats often eat penguin eggs and chicks.

Gathering guano

In some countries, people gather penguin guano and sell it as **fertilizer**. When too much guano is removed from an area, the penguins that make nests out of guano have nowhere to lay their eggs. Penguin populations decrease when the birds do not lay eggs. The population of Humboldt penguins has dropped from 50,000 to fewer than 15,000 because of guano gathering.

A history of hunting

For hundreds of years, people hunted penguins and gathered their eggs. Millions of penguins were hunted so people could make money by selling penguin skins and feathers. People made many products, including clothing and purses, from penguin skins. They used penguin feathers as stuffing for pillows and mattresses, and as decorations on clothing. Millions of penguins were also killed for their blubber, which was used to make oil for lamps.

Royal penguins were once endangered because of hunting. They are now protected, so the population of royal penguins has increased.

Protected penguins

Today, all seventeen species of penguins are protected by law. It is **illegal**, or against the law, to hunt penguins, gather penguin eggs, or to harm penguins in any way. Some people continue to kill penguins, however. People kill penguins for their meat, their feathers, their skins, or to use them as fishing **bait**. People also still gather penguin eggs for food.

In South America, people hunt Humboldt penguins for food and for fishing bait.

Commercial fishing

Commercial fisheries are businesses that catch and sell fish. Many commercial fisheries **overfish**, or take too many fish from, certain areas of the oceans. When the fish that penguins eat are overfished, penguins may not find enough food to survive.

25

Global warming

People burn huge amounts of **fuels** such as coal, oil, and gas to heat their homes, run their cars, and to get electricity. Burning these fuels contributes to **global warming**. Global warming is a rise in the temperature of Earth.

Melting ice and snow

Global warming causes the ice around Antarctica to melt and break apart. This melting is dangerous to some species of penguins. For example, some emperor penguins breed on huge sheets of pack ice. They breed far from the edges of the pack ice, so their chicks will be a safe distance from the ocean. If the pack ice breaks up before the chicks have fledged, the chicks may fall into the ocean and drown or freeze to death.

Warming oceans

Global warming causes ocean temperatures to rise. Even the freezing Southern Ocean is getting warmer. Warming oceans cause problems for many ocean animals, including penguins. One problem is that there are not as many krill in warm oceans as there are in cold oceans.

As the Southern Ocean warms, the amount of krill decreases. Most of the penguins that live around Antarctica feed mainly on krill, so many starve because they cannot find enough food.

Rockhopper penguins feed mainly on krill. They are vulnerable because there is not enough krill in the waters where they live.

People and penguins

Scientists around the world study penguins in their habitats. They study penguins to learn what the birds need to survive and how to protect them from becoming extinct. Scientists often put identification tags on penguins to record each penguin's movements and behaviors. The tags also allow scientists to track the number of penguins that live in a certain area. By counting penguins, scientists can find out which species are endangered.

Most penguins are not afraid of people, so scientists can get close to these animals in the wild to study them. These scientists are studying Adélie penguins.

Tourism

Each year, many **tourists** visit penguins in their habitats. After seeing penguins in the wild, people often want to protect them. Some of the money that tourists spend to visit penguins in the wild is used for research and **conservation**. Tourists must be careful to avoid disturbing penguins and their activities, however. They must also avoid damaging or polluting penguin habitats.

These tourists watch penguins from a distance. Being too close would disturb the birds.

Helping penguins

Conservationists are people who provide animals with safe places to live and have babies. They are working hard to conserve penguins and their habitats around the world. They help penguins by protecting the forests, beaches, and other natural areas where penguins make nests and raise chicks.

Warm while waiting

Conservationists rescue penguins that have been covered with oil from **oil spills**. They wash the penguins with warm soapy water. Once their feathers are clean, the penguins can then preen to make their feathers waterproof again. After the feathers are clean and waterproof, the penguins can return to their habitats. Penguins covered with oil are often too sick to be washed right away, however. To keep these penguins warm and to prevent them from preening their poisoned feathers, conservationists put warm wool sweaters on them! The sweaters are made and donated by volunteers around the world.

You can help, too!

Even though you may live far away from penguins, you can still help them from where you live. Encourage your family and friends to avoid using **pesticides** and other chemicals and never throw garbage into any bodies of water.

The chemicals and garbage end up in oceans around the world. Over time, they harm penguins and other ocean animals. You can also knit a sweater to keep an oil-covered penguin warm!

You can help penguins by cleaning the beaches near where you live.

Glossary

Note: Boldfaced words that are defined in the text may not appear in the glossary.

bait Food or other items that are used to catch fish

clear To remove all the plants from an area

conservation The action of preserving or protecting a species or habitat

contact call A sound a penguin makes to help it locate another penguin

equator An imaginary line around the center of Earth

fertilizer A substance that is added to soil to help plants grow

fuel A material that is burned to produce heat or power

oil spill Describes a large amount of oil that spills into an ocean or onto land

pesticide A chemical people spray on plants to kill insects

pollution Harmful materials, such as garbage or chemicals, which make water, soil, or air unclean

population The total number of one species of animal living in a certain area

predator An animal that hunts and eats other animals

prey An animal that is hunted and eaten by another animal

South Pole The most southern point on Earth

Southern Hemisphere The half of Earth that is south of the equator

tourist A person who travels for fun

waterproof Describes something that water cannot get through

wild Places in nature that are not controlled by people

Index

Printed in the U.S.A.